THE **TOPRA GUID**

GW01425253

Careers
IN REGULATORY AFFAIRS

EDITED BY

Jenine Willis

TOPRA
PUBLISHING

The TOPRA Guide to

Careers in Regulatory Affairs

Editor
Jenine Willis

Contributors
Susan Botfield, Tony Cartwright, Graham Donaldson, Ming
Ewe, Debbie Finlay, Paul Foster, Michael Holzhauser-Alberti,
Craig McCarthy, Angela Miller, Sarah Roberts, Heimo Scheer,
Davina Stevenson, Nick Sykes, Hilde Viroux, Lynda Wight

Copyright © TOPRA Publishing 2010

ISBN 978-0-9564943-1-3

www.topra.org

Designed by The Upper Room

Contents

Introduction

If you think a career in healthcare Regulatory Affairs could be for you, then this is the guide to read before you go any further! Due to popular demand TOPRA, the European Regulatory Affairs professional organisation, has pooled together a wide variety of experiences and advice from professionals who already work in Regulatory Affairs. Our contributors range from Vice Presidents with years of regulatory experience to professionals who have just started on the regulatory career ladder. We have perspectives from pharmaceuticals, medical technologies, veterinary, consultants and regulators. We also have input from a recruiter and a career coach.

Regulatory Affairs is an international endeavour and there are great opportunities to travel and work abroad. However, the country where you are based, type of company you work for or your specialty will shape your day-to-day working environment. Although our content is focused on the European regulatory sector, the diverse experiences of regulatory affairs share common threads as you will read.

This booklet is aimed at graduates and postgraduates looking to enter the healthcare regulatory world be it in pharmaceuticals, medical technologies or veterinary sectors. Whichever specialty you choose, this dynamic environment provides an interesting, challenging and rewarding career for those who have the drive, the right qualities and qualifications. The TOPRA Guide to Careers in Regulatory Affairs will help to get you on the right track and TOPRA itself can help to support you as you make your first steps in your new career. Students and recent graduates who are not working in Regulatory Affairs are eligible to take advantage of our Student membership which gives valuable access to networking and other career opportunities. For further information go to www.topra.org

I'd like to thank all our contributors for their input into this publication. Every one of them has supported TOPRA over the years and all are committed to supporting new entrants to the profession. Their tips and suggestions will be helpful, but they are not mandatory! We look forward to hearing your views and experiences in due course and sharing them on the TOPRA careers website.

Jenine Willis, *Director, TOPRA Publishing*

Why choose a career in Regulatory Affairs?

What is Regulatory Affairs and why would I want a career in it?

Davina Stevenson, *Principal Regulatory Affairs Officer, European Regulatory Affairs, Mundipharma Research*

What is Regulatory Affairs?

Regulatory Affairs (RA) developed globally because governments have responded to concern over public health and product safety in areas such as pharmaceuticals, veterinary medicines, medical devices and pesticides. Requirements were placed on manufacturers to conform to stringent safety-testing procedures and obtain a marketing authorisation (MA) before placing products on the market. The MA is simply a licence to sell a product in a particular country.

Companies that have products subject to such legislation have established specialist RA departments staffed by RA professionals whose job it is to keep track of the legislation in all the regions in which the company wishes to distribute its products. Such professionals also advise on the legal and scientific restraints and requirements, they collect, collate, evaluate scientific data and present registration documents (dossiers) to regulatory agencies, and carry out all the subsequent negotiations necessary to obtain and maintain licences for the products concerned (lifecycle maintenance).

Numerous job descriptions are emerging to describe RA professionals, including RA Officers, Regulatory Executives and more recently, and perhaps most controversially, Regulatory Scientists. Regardless of the title, the ultimate aim of Regulatory Affairs is to support the development and achieve registration of:

- the right products
- with the right labelling
- at the right price.
- at the right time
- in the right markets

Regulatory Affairs and the development process

Regulatory Affairs covers all areas of the product lifecycle (Figure 1); we support the activities from the very beginning of the research phases to the end of the product where the patent has expired and marketing and commercial colleagues may be looking for input to expand sales, eg with new formulation registrations.

Figure 1: Typical Regulatory Affairs tasks as the product develops (© Davina Stevenson 2010)

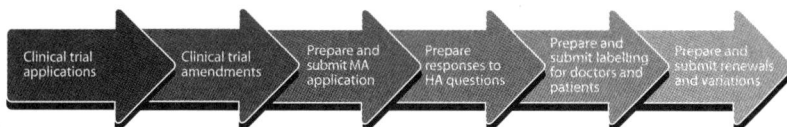

| Clinical trial applications | Clinical trial amendments | Prepare and submit MA application | Prepare responses to HA questions | Prepare and submit labelling for doctors and patients | Prepare and submit renewals and variations |

In order for a regulatory authority to be able to issue a MA, it must carry out a close scrutiny of all the technical reports generated during the development of the product and review the proposed manufacturing methods, quality control procedures and evidence of pharmacological activity, clinical safety and efficacy. This activity is known as 'assessment' and there is close contact between the assessors and the company RA staff involved with an application.

In broad terms, the assessor will critically review all the scientific evidence presented by the applicant company to establish that the product's quality, safety and efficacy are acceptable and that packaging and product claims are supported by this evidence. Product safety legislation is often subject to very rapid change in accordance with the development of scientific methods.

RA personnel must ensure that the product information submitted to the authorities is as complete as possible and in the correct style, layout and structure. They are also responsible for subsequent contacts with the regulatory authorities. Since authorisations are issued for a specified time, and have to be renewed before expiry, a very important part of the RA function consists of the maintenance and updating of existing authorisations, and in handling the inevitable 'variations' or changes in particulars that crop up from time to time.

It may take anything up to 15 years to develop and launch a new pharmaceutical product and many issues may arise in the process of scientific development. It is the job of the RA professional to help the company avoid deficiencies in their data which may create difficulties in the registration of the product. In most product areas where regulatory requirements are imposed, restrictions are also placed upon the claims which can be made for the product on labelling or in advertising. The RA department will consequently take part in the development of the product marketing concepts and is usually required to approve packaging and advertising before it is used commercially.

In general, Regulatory Affairs involves:
- Licensing, marketing and legal compliance of pharmaceutical and medical products
- A combination of science, legal and business – ensuring well-designed and validated data with appropriate statistics and discussions

- Devising and succinctly presenting a strategy for product registration
- Adherence and compliance to health authority (HA) guidelines and regulations
- A liaison role internally between research, production and business development and externally with HA personnel, inspectors and European regulators
- Information and intelligence gathering to try to anticipate change – keeping up-to-date with draft guidelines, European Directives and national laws and regulations.

Despite recent efforts towards harmonisation of requirements, there are differences between European, US and International (non-US) roles, the guidelines and timelines. There is normally a need to investigate local requirements for submission and although preparation is commonly based upon EU dossiers there are also regional or national style and format requirements which must be met. RA must devise efficient and economical research and development programmes where the results may be used as widely as possible in multiple regions. Pharmaceutical companies are heavy exporters of finished packed product and so the RA departments must be aware of the regulatory requirements in all the company's export markets. This may include import and export permits or obtaining licences for controlled drug substances and working with official bodies, such as the Home Office in the UK.

The Importance of the Regulatory Affairs function

The proper conduct of its RA activities may have considerable economic importance for the company concerned. In today's competitive environment the reduction of the time taken to reach the market is critical to a product's and hence the company's success. The presentation of an inadequate dossier may slow up the evaluation of a marketing application or even cause it to be rejected by the authorities. A new drug is likely to have cost many millions of dollars to develop over 15 to 20 years, and have a huge potential market. Any delay in bringing it to the market will have heavy financial consequences for the company and will deny a new treatment to patients. The RA department is often the first point of contact between the government authorities and the company so it plays an important public role.

Failures to fully report all the available data or the release of product bearing incorrect labelling may result in the need for a product recall. Either occurrence may lead to the loss of several millions in sales, not to mention the resulting reduction in customer and investor confidence. Rectifying inadequacies in the data submitted to the authorities can be very time-consuming and can add considerably to the expense of a project, to the extent of rendering it commercially non-viable.

The direct contribution of RA to the rest of the pharmaceutical business is demonstrated in Figure 2. This also means many interactions with different areas of the business and plenty of variety within the day-to-day tasks.

Figure 2: *RA contribution to the pharmaceutical business (© Davina Stevenson 2010)*

Reduce production cost and R&D spend	More and better new products
● Provide information and help to prepare post-marketing variations for different territories to implement manufacturing improvements, eg quicker analysis techniques and methods ● Prepare variations to add additional or replacement manufacturers to reduce manufacturing costs	● Participate in due diligence activities to develop portfolio and expand into new therapeutic areas ● Analyse business opportunities in terms of regulatory requirements and documents looking at competitor public assessment reports therapeutic guidance, regional variations in regulations and emerging legislation
Market expansion	**Strengthen market position**
● Support regulatory preparation of international or Eastern European (non-EU) submissions ● Gather advice from local contacts and prepare comparison to EU requirements	● Support regulatory development plan for generic and over-the-counter (OTC) lifecycle phases ● Prepare tailored training courses for commercial staff explaining the registration requirements

What is a typical day?

The daily tasks depend on the stage of the product lifecycle, eg, the project may be very early in the research and development stages and need clinical trial applications prepared, or it could be later on in post-approval when manufacturing changes may be needed (variations). This all leads to an interesting, dynamic and often complex but stimulating daily role.

Activities include:

● Dossier strategy and planning

● Preparation of MA Applications for submission via National or European Procedures in EU/EEA markets (eg, drafting quality, non-clinical and clinical expert reports and compilation of study reports)

● Preparation of responses to Health Authority questions within set and sometimes tight timelines

● Preparation and submission of licence variations

● Submission of licence renewals to maintain the right to market the product

● Provision of pharmaceutical, clinical and other technical information to other partners to help with their national requirements and licences

● Representation of the RA department on project teams for new product developments, providing regulatory advice as required

- Collection, collation and transfer of information and data into the internal registered product information databases
- Maintenance of records of regulatory actions in internal regulatory activity tracking systems.

All activities involve interaction internally within the different functions in the regulatory department, on cross-functional teams with other departments and externally with the health authorities (either on a national or regional basis). If you are seeking a job with lots of varied interactions then RA is perfect for you. We deal with almost every discipline within the industry eg, pharmacologists, toxicologists, analytical chemists, pharmacists, medical doctors, veterinarians, engineers, physical chemists and statisticians. There are also significant business and commercial interactions which make the job varied and interesting, eg, discussing projects with marketing, legal and business development colleagues.

This is an office-based job and there is no denying that there are a vast number of e-mails, telecons and meetings, but the hours are sociable and, unless there is a deadline, the workload manageable.

Why would I want a career in Regulatory Affairs?

A career in RA holds many advantages, possibilities and, commonly, challenges:

- Positive impact on society with registration of new drugs
- Dynamic environment
- Hybrid of science, business and communication
- Responsible socially ethical and moral job and business sector
- A practical application of science
- Diverse academic and industrial science backgrounds
- Good opportunity to progress and develop
- Opportunity to specialise (pharmaceuticals, compliance, operations, publishing, consultancy)
- Many different business areas, eg, medical devices, active ingredients, biopharmaceuticals, radio-pharmaceuticals
- Flexible working conditions (hours/locations, etc)
- Usually job stability and good terms.

Do I have the right qualifications and qualities for a regulatory career?

Angela Miller, *Director, Global Regulatory Affairs – Oncology and Haematology, Eisai*

First-timers

New entrants to Regulatory Affairs rarely have any knowledge of the legal frameworks, processes and procedures or standards required by the profession. These skills and those associated with the strategic thinking exhibited by senior professionals can be learned 'on the job', although this may take many years. In addition, because legislation changes frequently it is unlikely that any one person will possess all of the knowledge required at any time. Thus a commitment to continued learning and updating is essential throughout any career in RA at any level. Knowledge of the drug development process, the pharmaceutical industry and how it is regulated is very desirable. A newcomer to the profession can get an insight into these from websites and publications, however there is no substitute for experience.

Regulatory Affairs covers a broad spectrum of scientific disciplines. Most new entrants to the profession will possess a degree in a scientific discipline, such as Chemistry, Biology or Pharmacy as it is essential that the RA professional understands the products they are working on. However, because of the dynamic and ever-changing healthcare environment, an understanding of the market place is highly valued and degrees in subjects such as health economics and law are also useful. Higher degrees are advantageous but are not essential and can be achieved by attending courses on a part-time basis.

So-called 'soft skills' are extremely important and an ability in project management, scientific writing, negotiation and interpersonal and communication skills is highly valued. A 'can do' attitude and problem-solving approach to challenges is also highly advantageous. These skills together with a scientific background will allow the newcomer to be seen as credible at all levels, but particularly within the project teams with whom they will be working most of the time. It is also essential that the RA professional maintains a current level of knowledge, so a willingness to keep up-to-date with new procedures and initiatives is essential.

Progressing

As someone progresses through a career in RA they would be expected to learn about lifecycle management and start to combine the technical and scientific aspects of RA with project management and increased strategic thinking. These skills take time to acquire and as a guide this level is not usually reached until 5-8 years of solid regulatory grounding has been obtained. A professional will probably have been introduced to HA meetings earlier, but at this stage it is possible that they will be responsible for the planning and conduct of such meetings. A clear and concise communication style is now an essential part of the RA toolkit. It is important at this level to be able to blend the skills of knowing the guidelines with knowledge of the therapeutic area being studied, in order to apply the regulation to the condition being investigated in a meaningful manner.

At the highest level

After a further 5 years or so individuals can expect to be moving their focus to a more tactical level; integrating the regulatory knowledge gained into strategic planning. Individuals will need to have developed strong planning and management skills. They may also be involved in business-critical activities, so communication skills come to the fore as communicating change to all levels and disciplines, persuading teams to follow new legislation, staff development and vendor management are all critical tasks. As well as attending RA-related courses it is important that the regulatory professional is increasing their knowledge of the therapeutic area in which they are working – thus attendance at medical conferences becomes important.

At the highest level RA professionals are leaders and mentors. They have a strategic role and often play a part in policy development. They often interact with the regulators and internal and external policy-making groups at a high level. Again communication skills and a collaborative work ethic are essential together with experience of global regulations across many therapeutic areas.

In summary

If a career in RA still appeals, do you possess the following qualifications and qualities. If the answer is yes then a career in RA could be a very rewarding choice:

- a scientific background to understand the products and create credibility within project teams
- an ability to express complex ideas in simple understandable language
- a willingness to learn how to interpret regulations and guidelines and apply them to assigned projects
- an open mind
- a willingness to continue to learn and update knowledge
- flexibility and adaptability
- a collaborative spirit.

You've applied for an entry level job in Regulatory Affairs – how should you prepare for and behave at your interview?

Presentation: Eventually you could be the company's 'face' in front of the health authorities. Dress smartly but comfortably.

Background reading: Have a look at the relevant company's website. Get some background knowledge of the company. A prospective employer will always be impressed if you have done some homework. Take a look at some Health Authority websites. Most HAs around the world have a website, eg, the EMA and the US FDA. Have a look at the overviews rather than the actual legislation, you will not be expected to know about procedures and processes if you are new to RA. Having basic overview knowledge of how and why medicines are regulated will show a prospective employer that you know what RA is and have not just picked any job. If you have some understanding of the drug development process as well that is a definite bonus.

Preparation: Think about the qualities of a RA professional. Have you done anything where you have had to communicate clearly? Have you led a team, did you enjoy it, what were the difficulties? Have you ever been in a situation where you have had to be flexible and change your plans, what did you do?

At the interview: In the interview, the prospective employer will be looking for you to communicate clearly, this is essential for a RA professional. Speak up but don't shout, answer the questions asked, be concise. Think about the examples you prepared – are any of them relevant to the question being asked?

When taking on a new entrant into the profession, a prospective employer is looking for someone who is going to give something back to the company. Think about what skills you have to offer and bring them to the fore. The employer is looking for someone who can be flexible, can adapt to changing situations and someone who is willing to learn. If you don't know the answer to a question then say so, never pretend you know – be honest – you can always research that topic afterwards and if you have a second interview give the information at that point.

And finally, RELAX! The people who are interviewing you have almost certainly been in the same position as you in the past. Remember they are human too.

Getting started on your regulatory career

Securing your first regulatory role

Paul Foster, *Resource Manager - Regulatory Affairs, Quality Assurance and Health Economics, AXESS*

The healthcare industry is a highly regulated market and encompasses a wide range of disciplines including agrochemicals, animal health and medical devices. In this chapter we will be reviewing the career opportunities open to candidates entering the probably the largest sector of the biopharmaceutical industry for human health.

That critical first role!

Historically, Regulatory Affairs is an extremely difficult sector to break into straight from university as most RA professionals have gained experience in different roles within the industry before seeking a career within RA. It is true to say that most pharmaceutical companies are not looking to take on inexperienced candidates and are looking for RA professionals with a minimum of 18-24 months experience who can 'hit the ground running'. The exception to this are companies that run internships or development programmes, eg, where over a 2-year period you would undertake three placements within differing areas of RA giving you a broad understanding of the regulatory environment and regulatory process from development to commercialisation. These programmes are few and far between and competition for places is intense.

The options open to graduates are therefore limited to a few organisations that will invest in the training and development required for a new entrant to make a valuable contribution to the regulatory department and they can be broken down into three different groups, generics companies, CROs and regulatory consultancies. Your choice of entry into the pharmaceutical industry is likely to have a significant influence on your future career path as the experiences gained will vary from one group to another.

Here is a summary of what each group is looking for from a graduate or postgraduate and the likely career paths available:

Generic pharmaceutical companies

This is an extremely fast-paced, commercial environment and applicants will have to have had some work experience, ideally within the pharmaceutical industry, so sandwich courses with internships would be really useful. If this is not available then your choice of vacation work should enable you to demonstrate some of the core competencies required in an entry level role, such as time management and attention to detail. In this case your CV should be seen as a marketing tool to enable you to get an interview. You should tailor your CV and covering letter to match the job description and core competencies for the role; you should also be able to demonstrate an understanding of the product development and regulatory process for generic products. It goes without saying that your CV and covering letter should be free of any grammatical and spelling mistakes.

If you are fortunate enough to be interviewed, your interviewer will be looking to assess you against the core competencies and you will need to demonstrate how you have the experience on either a personal or work-related front that match these competencies.

If successful you will over time be exposed to many regulatory processes such as Chemistry, Manufacturing and Controls (CMC), MAs and variations and renewals for the older more established products. You are not going to be exposed to products within clinical development and this may restrict your career path to the generic Industry or to local affiliate roles within the wider pharmaceutical industry.

Contract research organisations

These were the traditional routes for graduates to gain their first role in RA. However, the market has changed and many CROs are suffering from cost pressures and a lack of resources, so are unable to invest the time and manpower required to train and develop a fresh graduate. This is compounded by the fact that the CRO will be unable to charge the client for your work while you are being trained. This means that they will be highly selective in their graduate recruitment and demand either a first class honours degree or MSc in one of the key scientific disciplines as a minimum entry level.

The core competencies required are similar to that of a generic company, however, candidates will be required to demonstrate an understanding of the phases of clinical development and how that impacts upon the regulatory process. This is also a fast-paced environment where time management and attention to detail are critical competencies. In this role, however, due to the lack of resources, candidates will have to be self-starters and be able to demonstrate how they will seek out the relevant information and get on with it!

CROs by their very nature concentrate their activity within the clinical development programme from Phase I through to Phase III and successful candidates may have a bias towards submission of clinical trial applications (CTAs). While *prima facie* this appears quite restrictive it is a skill set that many pharmaceutical companies require and there are likely to be opportunities to move across onto the client side and gain a wider range of regulatory knowledge. The optimal time to seek employment within pharmaceutical companies from a CRO background would be with 18-24 months' experience otherwise you tend to run the risk of becoming too specialised!

Regulatory Affairs consultancies

The issues within regulatory consultancies are very similar to a CRO, however, the good news is that there are some specialist consultancies that will invest in new talent straight from university. In fact there is one leading consultancy whose business model has been based on recruiting postgraduate talent and investing long-term in their personal development. As a result staff retention has been excellent – their beautiful if somewhat isolated location helps too!

The key differences with working for a consultancy, rather than a CRO or generics company, are that there is potential to be exposed to roles and procedures throughout the regulatory lifecycle from clinical development through to commercialisation. However, not all consultancies are the same and it is down to the individual to understand what the consultancy offers its clients and gain an insight into the training and development programme offered by the company. Otherwise you may become too specialised in one particular aspect of RA which may potentially affect your marketability to the pharmaceutical industry in the future. In addition the candidates will be working closely with clients and therefore will require excellent communication skills.

The long-term view

As previously discussed most regulatory professionals started their career in other roles within the pharmaceutical Industry before transferring into RA. The entry points have been extremely varied and range from laboratory-based work within the research function through to clinical development, pharmacovigilance and data management. In a lot of cases the entry criteria is lower and a good quality 2:1 or even 2:2 will enable you to secure a role.

Once you have established a good reputation within this role, this will be a minimum of 18-24 months, and have demonstrated the core competencies required within a regulatory role then you should start looking for an internal transfer. As with all the other roles your choice of entry into RA is critical for your career development. Choose well!

Routes into Regulatory Affairs

Ming Ewe, *Regulatory Consultant, Eureca Consulting, UK*

A wonderful way of stimulating conversation with regulatory professionals is to ask them how they came to be in Regulatory Affairs. No individual's answer is ever the same. Those who enter immediately after graduating from university tend to join small- to medium-sized pharmaceutical, generic or device-based companies. Of those who join later, most tend to have worked in the pharmaceutical or healthcare industry, typically in pharmacy, R&D, quality assurance (QA), quality control (QC), manufacturing and clinical departments. Occasionally some entrants have worked in veterinary or in pharmaceutical sales before their regulatory career. There is some anecdotal evidence that it may be possible to work in RA without a scientific background; however, the barrier to entry is much higher and career opportunities are limited. This is because some regulatory professionals believe that a good scientific degree is needed in order to be able to interpret scientific data, be sufficiently knowledgeable and equipped to handle the more interesting but demanding tasks, particularly regarding regulatory strategy.

It is therefore difficult to prescribe a one-size-fits-all approach to those wanting to start their RA career. It does mean, however, that there are a variety of ways into RA depending on how flexible, creative, and perhaps patient, you can be in terms of your entry strategy. It's therefore helpful to consider the following:

- The length of time you have been in education and the amount of relevant industry experience you have may govern how selective you can afford to be. The longer you have been in education with no relevant industry experience, the more you will have to demonstrate why you deserve the job and have commercial/industry awareness, especially as you will be competing against your more experienced peers. The contradiction is that although there is a general preference, particularly in the larger organisations, to employ senior RA professionals with at least an MSc or PhD, industry is generally suspicious of those who have studied or worked in academia for too long as they believe that they are out of touch with industry! However there are opportunities to encourage postgraduate students to become more entrepreneurial and to increase their awareness regarding the commercialisation process of bioscience ideas, such as the UK nationwide Biotechnology Young Entrepreneurs Scheme (YES) and the regionally focused Bioscience YES in Yorkshire and Humber areas of the UK (see www.biotechnologyyes.co.uk and www.bioscienceyes.co.uk).

- Can you gain exposure to RA by seeking employment in areas with easier access or lower competition or barriers to entry? Things to consider include:
  o Other industry sectors – agrochemical, cosmetics, veterinary or generics
  o Types of role within RA depending on the organisational structure of the department – regulatory operations, regulatory project management, regulatory intelligence
  o Other geographical RA regions – instead of applying for FDA and European centralised regional RA roles which are very competitive, target international RA instead. However, this option has become popular lately with the increasing growth of emerging markets such as Brazil, Russia, India and China (also known as BRIC countries)
  o Geographical location – some organisations may have CMC RA groups located at their manufacturing site(s) rather than at headquarters or in centralised regional offices. Furthermore employers in some geographical locations find it harder to recruit and may be more open-minded about the types of candidate they might consider.
- What is your preferred way of working? Do you prefer performing a variety of tasks (breadth) or performing a few tasks but repeatedly over time so that you become akin to an expert (depth)? In consultancies, CROs, small companies and small national affiliate offices, the RA role is typically extremely varied with exposure to different regulatory procedures over the course of the product lifecycle compared to that in a large blue-chip organisation where RA roles may be much more compartmentalised and thus specialised.
- Do you understand what RA is and the registration process in your target industry sector? This knowledge will help you to identify less well-publicised routes into RA such as:
  o Regulatory agencies or institutions, eg, the EDQM, which is responsible for establishing quality standards for human and veterinary medicinal products and is involved in consumer health protection programmes
  o Other stakeholders, such as charities, universities and hospitals which may run or be involved with clinical trials, such as Cancer Research UK.
- Apart from keeping abreast of new developments in RA for interview purposes, it may also help you to identify new opportunities for employment. Often when there is an introduction of a new or changed regulatory requirement or legislation, this has resulted in an increase in workload and demand for resources, and eventually an increase in employment. One example of this is the increasing move towards e-submissions during the past decade, particularly regarding the eCTD .

● Consider the key skills or qualities that are required for a RA professional, such as attention to detail and report writing, especially those skills which may be your weakest. If you have currently been unsuccessful in securing a RA role, can you develop these skills in another capacity in the meantime to improve your chances later?

As many outsiders to RA have pointed out, they frequently face a Catch-22 situation: employers often demand RA professionals have some experience, however there are few opportunities to obtain such experience. A few of the large blue-chip companies, such as GlaxoSmithKline and Pfizer sometimes offer industrial placements and graduate trainee schemes. Anecdotally it appears that fewer internships are offered in industry compared with regulatory agencies and institutions, such as the US FDA, EMA and EDQM.

To summarise, for those thinking about how to enter the RA field:
● There are many different routes into RA, some directly or indirectly after university.
● Although there are very few internships or graduate trainee schemes, they do exist!
● Being flexible, creative and patient is key to determining and planning your entry strategy
● If you have been unsuccessful in securing an RA role this time round:
○ Identify what skills and attributes are key for an RA professional
○ Perform a gap analysis of your own skills and attributes
○ Plan how to strengthen them in another role or capacity to improve your chances of securing a RA role later.

For those in industry, regardless of whether you have responsibilities for hiring and managing staff or not:
● General awareness of RA as a potential scientific career is still lacking. What can we do to help?
● How can we create opportunities to help future recruits gain RA experience so that we can pass the baton on to them?

Last, but not least, at a fundamental level, this begs the bigger question: how can we encourage more people to consider or remain in science as a career?

*This chapter was written using various sources of literature and careers' surveys. References are available on request.

Preparing for a regulatory career – find your springboard

Graham Donaldson, *Senior Regulatory Affairs Executive, TRAC Services*

Regulatory Affairs is a career where you can use the knowledge and skills gained at university. It is often an over-looked career path within the pharmaceutical and healthcare sectors losing out to more well-known job options. However, for those graduates who get the opportunity, RA roles provide a varied, interesting, ever-evolving and extremely rewarding career. One day you may be looking at scientific data, chairing meetings or giving presentations. The next you may be on a flight to meet a new client or start a new project.

What really hits home when you start working in RA is that the work you do directly contributes to helping safeguard the health and well-being of many millions of people across the world. The pharmaceutical industry relies on those people within the RA profession, as do the people using the products.

It is because of the importance of the role that recruiters look for not only academic achievement but a mature attitude and a wide range of transferable skills. RA roles will need a good grasp of science. Traditionally people going into RA would have a background in pharmacy, however now RA opportunities are opening up to a wider range of people. Job adverts will typically want a degree in Biological Sciences or Chemistry or allied discipline. Many will say that a further degree or post-graduate qualifications in RA would be beneficial. However, other degrees may not be discounted.

From day one you will be liaising with clients or other departments within your organisation, therefore people with other work experience will be looked upon more favourably. RA is one profession that never stands still, there is something new to learn every day.

While training opens you up to the wider issues concerning the profession, RA is a very client-focused job and the real learning and knowledge comes from 'hands on' project work. Unless you have done specific RA modules at undergraduate level or have post-graduate qualifications you will soon realise that you will have a whole new language to learn!

Getting a foot on the ladder

There is a lot of useful advice on the TOPRA careers website for people looking to get into RA. TOPRA has a working group whose role it is to bring RA to an undergraduate audience, through closer working links with universities, to explain the opportunities that exist within RA.

Graduates looking to get into the profession should look to do the basics well. Sign up with one of the many RA recruitment specialists and produce a good CV, emphasising the key points you have learned in your studies and that are relevant to RA. Do your research about RA, especially topics about the pharmaceutical industry that are currently in the news. Nobody will expect you to know everything about a hugely diverse field, but it will show your interest and willingness to learn.

As in any career path, there is no substitute for a positive attitude and enthusiasm. These are the qualities that will make you stand out. You can learn about RA and the pharmaceutical industry but you will need to show commitment to take the opportunities that will come your way. Work experience is invaluable but can be hard to get. Although it may seem like taking another year before you graduate, taking a sandwich year placement may be a good idea, and in the long term taking this approach can be extremely beneficial.

Opportunities

Regulatory Affairs is such a diverse profession and offers a wealth of opportunities for the people working within it, whether in one of the large multinational pharmaceutical companies or in the growing number of smaller regulatory consultancies that work with pharmaceutical companies who are increasingly looking to outsource their RA requirements, rather than have in-house teams. There are also companies like medical device or software companies which require RA in order to market their products.

The type of organisation will also define a lot of the kind of work you will do. It may be difficult to differentiate between companies, so it is worth looking at the types of work they do, as there are many varied roles undertaken in RA. Working for a small consultancy will be very different to being in a department of a multinational organisation or a government regulatory agency and each will provide different opportunities.

RA will draw on the scientific and legal knowledge gained at University, but you will constantly be building on those skills. You may become an expert in an area you had never heard of before you started your career. If you are working for a smaller consultancy you may also be involved in other business areas.

You will be working with highly qualified colleagues, whose experience, expertise and understanding of the industry will be an invaluable resource for you, so tap into that knowledge base and use it for your own development.

Moving into RA from other departments

RA sits at the heart of the pharmaceutical industry and as a result RA professionals have interactions with other professions throughout the drug development lifecycle. RA professionals will typically interact with quality, logistics, project management and clinical teams among others. There are a number of different departments within a pharmaceutical company which will give you an understanding of RA and an appreciation of the breadth of knowledge required for the pharmaceutical industry. RA covers a lot of varied areas, so allied experience will put you in good stead for future RA opportunities. It is worth looking for opportunities within other pharmaceutical departments – as it will then be easier to move into a RA role.

Regulatory agencies, such as the MHRA in the UK, also offer opportunities. In a recent TOPRA survey of regulatory professionals with 2-5 years experience, 16% had previous experience within a regulatory agency (see www.topra.org).

For work within CMC, you will require a good understanding of the quality aspects of RA. Therefore work within QA or a QC lab will provide valuable experience and knowledge to step into an allied RA role. This may be with regulatory manufacturing compliance or their colleagues in a central regulatory function. In the same survey this was the most popular route into RA, with 17.5% already having had experience in a quality role. The second most popular route was via a scientific discipline: 17% of the people surveyed came from a scientific background that was either analytical, formulation or research-based.

Clinical roles are another way of gaining valuable experience. These could involve working in medical writing, research or clinical trials. Pharmacovigilance, the study of the safety of marketed medicines, is a rapidly expanding area of RA (see page 26).

Major international pharmaceutical companies sometimes have graduate development schemes. These usually involve around 2 years of on-the-job training, rotating between different departments for 6 months.

Smaller RA consultancy companies offer graduate development schemes. As the pharmaceutical industry moves to outsource more work, there will be more opportunities within consultancy firms. There are also university-led schemes that can place postgraduates within an organisation for a year after graduation. These can be excellent schemes and are worth researching and looking out for because they will give you both experience and an opportunity to be mentored through the learning process.

International opportunities – regional differences

Sarah Roberts, *Senior Director Regulatory Affairs, Celerion, and* **Heimo Scheer**, *Vice President Regulatory Affairs, Celerion*

The opportunity to work in global Regulatory Affairs, crossing regional boundaries, can be very challenging but these challenges provide the rewards and thrills that drive an RA professional's career. RA is a wonderful mix of medical sciences, manufacturing, marketing, and human behaviour. It is in the international environment that the subjective nature of the human behaviour aspect comes right into the forefront because your successful filing of a clinical trial or MA will be directly dependent also on your understanding of local politics, customs, and mores. How else can one explain why one hard scientific fact can result in such divergent opinions and, therefore, regulatory consequences in different regulatory jurisdictions? In this short chapter we hope to describe how your regulatory career and, by extension, the company you work for can profit from the challenges of working in a global environment.

Whether you work in the US, Europe or elsewhere there are set procedures governed by law, guidances, and precedent which define the interactions with the competent authorities. From the preparation of documents for submission to process of submission and review, there is a wealth of information available. However, these procedures generally cover the hard facts of the processes but rarely cover the softer cultural aspects of those interactions, ie, is it appropriate to phone a particular agency and check on the progress of your application? Accessing, understanding, and expertly interpreting this information is critical in successfully working across different regions.

The most direct source of information is on the regulatory agency websites. Care must taken since the quality and currency of the website information varies from agency to agency, and don't forget that the local language of the website may not be a language you are intimately familiar with and you may not be able to understand the nuances. Also not forgotten should be that the regulatory mantra of 'if it is not written, it does not count', will not apply in many cases. In fact, a phone call to an agency can quickly reveal that the deadline you have been worrying about is far more flexible (or rigorous, if you are not so lucky) than defined on the webpage. There are also unwritten practices that you will not know until you have committed a transgression of some sort. Regulatory judgement and prudence should mitigate against any major calamity, but it is only with experience and properly learning from that experience that the RA professional can move all submissions forward adequately and effectively.

Many companies with a global footprint utilise their local resource for working with the agencies for this reason. Some use this resource merely as an information portal, translating the information for a central resource, whereas others use these local resources much more during the submission process. Indeed in certain countries, having a native language speaking representative in the territory concerned is essential in carrying out these interactions with the agencies. While written documentation in English is largely acceptable across nearly all jurisdictions with major exceptions in some Asian countries (but please note, for obvious reasons informed consent forms always must be available in the language of the patient), verbal interactions are best carried out by those fluent in the local language, even in major European countries.

While most information can be gathered direct from websites or from experience in working in that territory, there are a number of database providers who can provide extensive regulatory intelligence across the different regions. These sources of information can be extremely valuable to smaller companies who do not have local presence. Understanding where this information can be found, and who in your company you can approach to help you in implementing the information, is vital in working across a global marketplace. If working in a small company without a local presence, the RA professional will increase their managerial expertise by overseeing the tactical operations and the overall strategies of the external locally based RA expertise.

Challenges of working across territories

Let us consider some of the challenges that we may face when working across territories. In this example, we are working on the initial submission for a global Phase III clinical study with sites in Europe, Asia, and North and Latin America. The company concerned is manufacturing a product in Europe and the brand comparator product is marketed in the US. The list below is by no means exhaustive but can show some of the differences:

- What is the global trial submission strategy? Are submissions in waves of countries? Is there a key country to target the first approval from?
- How will the proposed Phase III trials support the ensuing commercial registration strategy?
- Essential document requirements – what does each country need?

- Translations, original signatures, notarised documents and local documents specific for individual countries may be needed
- Who is preparing the documents for approval? When will the documents be available?
- Procedures for submission (CD or paper? How many copies? Are there special binders? Can it be mailed or does it need to be hand delivered?)
- What are timelines to regulatory approval so that time to first dosing can be effectively scheduled?
- How are requests for further information going to be handled?
- Amendments (global or local) - how will they be handled?
- Coordination with global and regional project managers and clinical leads
- Coordination with local country support
- Last-minute updates or requirements from the regulatory agency
- Agency payments - how much, when and to whom?

For most RA professionals, the starting point in their career will be in a role which is limited by its territorial jurisdiction. Typically companies cluster together in countries into regions and have small teams of professionals who are responsible for managing the regulatory aspects in those countries. This is particularly true at the development through to marketing stage whereby a team of RA professionals may be utilised for coordinating the European submissions for a large global Phase III study or responsible for marketing activities for a particular drug product, say, in Latin America.

Many companies today foster the development of the RA professional's career by allowing and encouraging cross-jurisdictional activities. While final responsibility for any submission would typically reside with the local function, exposure to and assumption of select RA responsibilities into another jurisdiction should greatly stimulate the interest and career of both a recent entrant as well as an experienced RA professional. Roles where knowledge of global RA is required are increasingly becoming more commonplace. This can take many forms: from the informal approach of casual, *ad hoc* questions to formal questions related directly to regulatory activities on the critical path of drug development or commercial registration. In either case, there may well be the opportunity to work on applications for different countries because of overflow from existing smaller teams in that organisation. This not only increases the individual's skill set but can also strengthen team relationships and allow for understanding of the processes cross-territory. A more formal approach would be to have a centralised global strategy and operations team responsible for all submissions and strategy worldwide but even here, a fine-tuned understanding of the local regulatory environments and, if not certain, to whom the local questions need to be addressed, are a burgeoning part of the RA professional's armamentarium.

Practical implications

Working globally can be very rewarding but some basic working principles differ across territories which the RA professional should appreciate and accommodate to allow effective collaborations. These include:

- Time-zone differences (ie, coordinating calls with multiple time-zones, such as West Coast USA – UK – Japan)
- Cultural differences (style, values, mores, beliefs)
- Holiday differences (European summer extended holiday versus shorter more frequent US holidays)
- Working-time practices
- Language differences - try to avoid colloquialisms and idioms
- Conflict resolution
- Decision making

Personal implications

With knowledge of a particular territory, there are opportunities available for RA professionals to work abroad either working on a territory that is familiar to them or in that new territory. This can be an exciting opportunity to broaden your skill set, enhance your career, understand a new culture and maybe learn a new language. Moving abroad can be a difficult decision but listed below are some considerations which may influence your decision:

- Do I need a visa to work in this new country? If so, will my company sponsor my visa application?
- How will my family be impacted by the change in country?
- Is there a relocation service within my organisation?
- What is my holiday entitlement?
- What are the expected working hours per week?
- Are all the public holidays in the new country recognised by my organisation?
- Will my pension/benefits/tax be affected by the move?
- Am I anticipating the move to be permanent or temporary?
- Am I entitled to local healthcare coverage?

In conclusion, RA is a great career choice if you enjoy working with multinational teams, and it can also offer the opportunity to work overseas.

Future opportunities – evolving regulatory specialties

Debbie Finlay, *Regulatory Affairs Executive, TRAC Services*

The Regulatory Affairs department within a company is responsible for all interactions with health authorities. The department is involved throughout a product's lifecycle from the time it is first tested in clinical trials, through to its launch on to the market until it finally leaves the market, generally because it has been superseded by a newer and more effective medical treatment. Throughout this process the RA team interacts with all the line functions responsible for generating the data included in regulatory findings. Today there are more specific areas that are evolving in the RA department. This chapter outlines a selection of these evolving specialties.

Regulatory intelligence

Regulatory intelligence (RI) is typically a task for a small group of specialists who are knowledgeable in all sources of regulatory information relevant to a specific company and the development of their medicinal products (see page 34).

It is the act of gathering and analysing regulatory information and monitoring the current regulatory climate. This intelligence enables the regulatory professional to create a strategy, a development plan and advise personnel on regulatory requirements now and in the future.

The role of an RI professional is to monitor the regulatory environment by keeping up to date with the ever-changing regulations and guidelines. There are many ways in which this can be performed from the screening of literature via electronic libraries and the internet, maintaining a database or repository for relevant guidelines, by distributing information within the organisation, and also by evaluating and interpreting guidelines for the company. However there is more to RI than just knowing the guidelines, it requires the ability to capture, process and effectively use information from such a variety of sources. At an advanced level RI professionals are able to influence evolving regulations by actively participating in the working parties that develop the guidelines and commenting on draft guidance documents. Acquiring and maintaining RI is the most important activity to a successful regulatory department.

Health Technology Assessment

Health Technology Assessment (HTA) is a multidisciplinary process that evaluates the efficacy, safety and cost-effectiveness of new treatments in a systematic, transparent and neutral manner. Its aim is to enable the introduction of effective patient-focused health policies by taking a scientific approach.

HTA can be used in many ways to advise or inform technology-related policy-making, for instance in regulatory agencies such as the MHRA, about whether to permit the commercial use of a drug, device or other technology. As a result HTA can help policy-makers decide which technologies are effective and which are not, and define the most appropriate indications for their use. HTA can also reduce or even eliminate interventions that are unsafe and ineffective or whose cost is too high compared with the benefits.

The regulatory process requires the agency to assess a new medicine on the basis of safety, quality and efficacy only and the legislation does not permit the consideration of price or cost-effectiveness (either absolute or relative to alternative treatments) to be part of the process of granting a marketing authorisation. Traditionally these aspects would be considered after the approval of an MA, usually by totally separate government departments, and dealt with by company departments outside RA.

With increasing pressure on healthcare budgets, the HTA process has become more common, with countries establishing national bodies to do this, such as the National Institute for Health and Clinical Excellence (NICE) in the UK. The deliberations of these bodies often include a review of the clinical data generated by the company that they have submitted as part of the MA process, so a link between the MA and HTA evaluations has been established. Clearly, it is therefore more efficient - and better from an ethical standpoint - if the clinical development programme for a new medicine takes account of the fact that data for HTA assessment will need to be developed, so that it does not have to be done later at more cost and with more patient trial exposure. Similarly, if companies approach regulatory agencies for formal Scientific Advice during the development process, this advice will have to bear in mind some of the HTA evaluations, if it is to be good advice.

For these reasons, regulatory professionals now have to grasp the principles of HTA assessment and understand for each EU country (at present the structure is not harmonised), when and how HTA evaluations are performed, and by whom. It is likely that this dimension of the process of delivering excellent treatment to the market place will become a regulatory specialty in its own right in the near future.

Pharmacovigilance

While the disaster of thalidomide brought about changes in the guidelines and laws concerned with drug development, it also brought with it a new era of drug safety monitoring.

Pharmacovigilance (PV) is the science relating to the detection, assessment, understanding and prevention of adverse effects, particularly long-term and short-term effects of medicines. This involves monitoring the use of medicines in everyday practice, being able to identify changes in the pattern of adverse effects and recognising any new adverse effects, while assessing the risks and benefits of medicines in order to determine if any action is required to improve their safety, and monitoring the impact of such action. This process of pharmacovigilance is quite complex and requires detailed plans and processes, structured activities, fixed responsibilities and regulated responses (see www.pipaonline.org).

Safety information is the basic aim in PV. It is the currency passed between parties and through systems and is what all outcomes and decisions are based on. The aim of a PV system is to capture the information, process it, evaluate it and pass it on to the necessary destinations. Any event can affect the risk–benefit assessment of a drug product. This includes not only adverse drug reactions but also information from use in pregnancy and other special populations (eg, the elderly, children or those with hepatic or renal impairment), instances of misuse, misadministration and overdose. This information can come from a variety of sources, such as the spontaneous reporting of adverse drug reactions, from clinical and epidemiological studies, from published literature, from regulatory agencies and from morbidity and mortality databases. The pharmaceutical company that holds the licence for the product (the MA holder) must work proactively to capture this information for all products that it is responsible for.

A new medicine has to pass through many hurdles before it is approved by the regulatory authority. Adequate evidence is required to show the new drug to be of good quality, effective and safe, although the quality and effectiveness must first be met before any consideration can be given to approve the drug. However the safety is not an absolute, and can only be judged in relation to how effective the drug is. This requires judgement from the regulators in deciding on acceptable limits of safety. There is always a possibility that rare but serious side-effects will not be detected in the initial safety testing. For example a fatal blood dyscrasia (abnormal blood components) occurring in 1 in 5,000 patients treated with a new drug is only likely to be recognised after 15,000 patients have been treated and observed. Such careful safety monitoring is not confined to new drugs or significant therapeutic advances. It also has an important role to play in the introduction of generic medicines, and in review of the safety profile of older medicines already available, where new safety issues may have arisen. It is as a result of this safety monitoring that drugs are sometimes withdrawn from the market after their initial approval.

Throughout the past decade we have seen an increase in the way drugs are marketed and used. Globalisation, consumerism, the explosion in free trade and communication across borders, the increasing use of the internet have all resulted in a change in access to all medicinal products and information on them. Such changes have given rise to new kinds of safety concerns, such as the illegal sale and abuse of drugs, an increase in self-medication practices, the widespread manufacture and sale of counterfeit and substandard drugs and the increased use of a combinations of medicines both traditional and herbal which have the potential for drug interactions. Drug safety monitoring is an essential element for the effective use of medicines and for high-quality medical care. It builds confidence and trust among patients and healthcare professionals in medicines while contributing to raising the standards of medical practice. Pharmacovigilance is a clinical discipline in its own right, and one that contributes to an ethos of safety and serves as an indicator of the standards of clinical care practices within a country.

However, the regulatory professional must understand the principles of PV in order to work with the experts in this area to produce periodic safety updates and to assess the impact of new safety information on product labelling and other literature.

Biocide legislation

While so far we have discussed the use of regulations in relation to medicines and medical technology, another evolving area is that of biocide legislation and biocide product regulation.

The Biocidal Products Directive (BPD) is implemented into UK law through the Biocidal Products Regulations (BPR). It requires that all biocidal products containing active substances be authorised if companies intend for them to remain/place them on the market. The regulating authority for Biocidal products in the UK is the Health and Safety Executive (HSE).

The BPD defines biocidal products as 'active substances and preparations containing one or more active substances, put up in the form in which they are supplied to the user, intended to destroy, deter, render harmless, prevent the action of or otherwise exert a controlling effect on any harmful organism by chemical or biological means'.

The main objectives for BPR are to harmonise the European market for biocidal products and their active substances, so that product authorisation in one European country can be recognised in another. The aim is also to provide a high level of protection for people, animals and the environment from the use of biocidal products through risk assessments. This will require the submission and evaluation of data relating to chemistry, toxicity to humans and the environment. Additionally, the BPR aims to ensure that products are sufficiently effective against the target species.

There are 23 different biocidal product types such as disinfectants, preservatives, pest control and speciality biocides ie, antifouling products and embalming fluids. However the BPD does not apply to products where its use is already regulated under certain other European legislation including plant protection products, human medicines, veterinary medicines, medical devices and cosmetics.

In June 2009, the European Commission adopted a proposal for a regulation concerning the placing on the market and use of biocidal products (COM(2009)267) This proposed regulation will repeal and replace the Directive 98/8/E and come into force on 1 January 2013.

Conclusion

Throughout this chapter we have briefly discussed some evolving regulatory specialisms, from regulatory intelligence, to safety assessments, drug monitoring to new guidelines and regulations. However, when all is said and done, these are all here to increase public safety.

Perspectives from regulatory professionals

Developing safer and more effective cancer treatments

Jon Wong, *Vice President Global Regulatory Affairs – Oncology and Haematology, Eisai*, talks to his colleague Angela Miller about his career in RA

Jon Wong was born in Malaysia but is now a naturalised British citizen. He has worked in the field of Regulatory Affairs for about 18 years and is currently Global Vice President of Oncology and Haematology RA at Eisai. After gaining a degree in Pharmacy and a PhD in Formulation of an Antineoplastic Agent, Jon started his career in formulation research and development before moving to the UK Medicines Control Agency (now the MHRA) to be a principal assessor of CMC for biotechnology and biological drugs. Since then Jon has worked at SmithKline Beecham and Chugai before moving to Eisai. Jon admits to having known nothing about the profession of RA before working as a formulation scientist but always knew that his interests lay within the medical science field and an education in pharmacy offered him a defined career path which allowed him to pursue his scientific inclinations.

As for what he enjoys most about RA, Jon says 'No two days are the same and the job allows interaction with many functions within an organisation – it teaches you vital skills of dealing with different people from marketers who are generally very dynamic and outgoing to the more introvert and conservative individuals from other functions.'

In his current role there is not one aspect which he likes more than another but feels all of the projects bring their own challenges and rewards. So what qualities and educational prerequisites does Jon consider crucial for a RA professional? 'A scientific background to understand the products and create credibility within project teams, an open mind, flexibility, adaptability and a collaborative spirit are all essential.'

So is there a tedious or negative side to the job which Jon would like to share? 'As with any job, there are mundane tasks that have to be done such as filing and, because pharmaceuticals are so highly regulated, SOP reading, writing and reviewing. The job has crunch periods which mean people sometimes have to work long hours which can impact on work-life balance which is not ideal, but then there is the reward of seeing a project completed.' As it appears the positives outweigh the negatives, would Jon recommend a career in RA? 'Yes it is a challenging, stimulating and rewarding profession where one will learn to perform a variety of tasks and gain a broad experience within the healthcare arena.'

As for the future – where are the new challenges in RA? He believes there are four main areas: paediatrics, the need to simplify clinical trials approvals in Europe, how to facilitate collaboration between regulatory and health technology assessment bodies and finally what quantitative methodology should be used in benefit–risk assessments.

Harnessing medical technologies for better healthcare

Hilde Viroux, *Associate Director, EU Medical Device RA, Alcon*

In the mid-1980s, medical devices were barely regulated, so, in common with many people currently in medical technology Regulatory Affairs, I didn't start my career in regulatory 25 years ago.

My first 'confrontation' with regulatory requirements occurred when I started with Alcon, at that time mainly a pharmaceutical company. Being responsible for Supplier Quality Management I would audit suppliers and contract manufacturers according to pharmaceutical GMP requirements.

When in 1993 the Medical Devices Directive (MDD) was published, I helped my company to set up and maintain the Quality Management System required by the MDD and became more familiar with regulatory requirements for medical technology products.

I became even more involved with medical technology RA when Alcon set up a kit-packing operation in Belgium. As the QA manager, it was my responsibility to ensure that products and processes met regulatory requirements and that the kits could be CE marked. I was also the contact person for the Notified Body, ie, the body that is authorised by the regulator, during the annual audits. It was difficult to obtain information at that time. Most of the regulatory requirements were learnt by self-study of the legislation and via discussions with the Notified Body.

By 2004 I had become fully involved with medical technology RA. The typical RA professional will usually be responsible for assembling the technical documentation, clinical evaluation, conformity assessment, applying the CE marking, and dealing with the Notified Body and authorities in the pre- and post-market phase.

My current job however, may not be representative of a medical technology regulatory professional. My responsibilities focus on the development of new legislation at the European level, and trying to influence future legislation. This means that I'm heavily involved with trade associations and representing industry in the different working groups related to medical technology in the European Commission, such as the Medical Devices Expert Group and the Borderline and Classification Group.

As a medical technology regulatory professional, you have to be aware not only of the MDDs, but also of other legislation affecting medical technology, like the machinery directive and the directive on personal protective equipment. Many legal instruments developed to protect the environment will also affect medical devices, like the legislation on Registration, Evaluation, Authorisation of Chemicals (REACH), the directive on Waste Electric and Electronic Equipment (WEEE), and the directive on Restriction of Hazardous Substances (RoHS).

Standards play an important part in medical technology, as harmonised standards are used to demonstrate conformity to the Essential Requirements of the MDDs. A medical technology regulatory professional needs to keep track of the harmonised standards and ideally will be aware of new developments in standardisation and other regulatory developments.

The area of medical technology is in full development. As medical technologies become more and more complex, so does the job of the medical technology regulatory professional. Future prospects are exciting in this branch of healthcare science.

Promoting improvements in animal health

Michael Holzhauser-Alberti, *Anses (formerly Afssa, the French veterinary regulatory agency)*

I remember the fast-food commercial slogan from my adolescence 'Where's the beef?' However, I never thought that the safety of that beef depended on regulators, and now it has been over 10 years since I started work in the Pharmaceuticals Assessment Unit at the French National Agency for Veterinary Medicinal Products (ANMV-Anses in Fougeres). Throughout my studies at Cornell Veterinary School, my interest in pharmacology and basic pathology and physiology developed and never let up, and thus, once I was in France, it wasn't by accident that I ended up at the ANMV, formerly part of AFSSA (the

French Food Safety Agency) and now Anses, which combines AFSSA and AFSSET (the French Environmental and Occupational Health Agency).

We regulators are desk warriors. When we assess an MA dossier for quality, safety, and efficacy, this can sometimes comprise processing more than 100 volumes, and perhaps what has changed the most over time is the amount of information that needs processing. This seems to be the case in many walks of life and holds true in the regulatory environment where the amount of scientific information available doubles every 10 years. When I started work as a regulator, generalised e-mail usage among member states was in its infancy. Many of the first MA procedures I managed at the European level still required the sending of faxes regularly. The French and European agencies have been at the forefront of information technology in order to stay afloat in this fast changing environment. Every day we are confronted with the paradox of making sense of superfast e-mails at the same time as we try the ins and outs of legislation many years in the making.

You might wonder if innovation can really be encouraged by something as dry as legislation. As regulators, we are privileged to answer positively here, and we try to support innovation where ever we can. Exchanging points of view, debating the latest research results, are an important part of my daily routine as I interact with veterinary scientists from our neighboring laboratory (Anses-Fougeres) or those at other Anses laboratories throughout France (eg, Ploufragan, also in Brittany) or at the French veterinary schools

There is a fundamental difference between benefit–risk assessment on the human and veterinary medicinal side, in that mass treatment is the mainstay where animals are group-housed and can often not be treated any other way, it is important to evaluate the impact of veterinary drugs, not only on animals and on humans, but also in the environment. Moreover, my colleagues in the Immunological Assessment Unit, through their work on biologically active substances, study disease containment. Then there are a number of points in common:

- There was a big effort to harmonise human and veterinary medicinal legislation with the Review of Legislation 2000
- A massive arrival of generic drug submissions forced us to change our view of what a medicinal product is and how to focus on the most critical aspects of a medicinal product
- There are areas where the smaller veterinary sector has so much to learn from the human sector: e-submissions, anticancer therapy, biotechnology, and so on. It is clear that veterinary and human sectors need to remain permeable

- The risk of antimicrobial resistance development is shared, and our responsibilities for doing something about it are also shared; veterinary regulators have been highly proactive in optimising treatments and remain as active as possible in limiting the development of further resistance, relying on new strategies.

The ever-important role of the EMA, located in London, must be underlined. I've been active there, as the French alternate CVMP member, since 2004, and my second mandate as chairman of the Efficacy Working Party is coming to fruition. Not only is going to London part of my great European adventure, but so is coming back to Fougeres whereby I can make sense of it all with my colleagues at the office, not far from grazing dairy cows!

It takes time for the task of the regulator to develop. First, one must understand the basics of each risk. Sometimes you have the luck to follow one risk in particular, and you develop specialist expertise. Then you need to weigh one risk against another in order to conclude your assessment and, in the process, prepare the basis upon which the MA decision is taken.

The inside track – working in regulatory intelligence

Nick Sykes, *Director, Regulatory Policy and Intelligence, Pfizer*

The combination of a regulatory intelligence (RI) and regulatory policy role requires me to maintain and develop a wide knowledge of the regulatory environment and understand the key elements of regulatory strategies being followed by our product teams. In addition, having an external focus necessitates the development of networks with colleagues outside Pfizer (through organisations such as TOPRA). The role also requires that I am recognised as speaking with authority and knowledge on Pfizer's positions both externally at conferences and other networking events, and internally with senior leaders.

When I first started in Regulatory Affairs nearly 20 years ago, regulatory intelligence was a relatively new concept with a smaller remit. Like many in RA, I have a science degree and have always wanted to work in the pharmaceutical industry; however, I did not want to be lab-based. After graduation, I considered working in RA but moved towards the information area. Having obtained a masters degree in Information Science I joined a small Regulatory Information team at SmithKline Beecham Pharmaceuticals (SB - now GlaxoSmithKline).

Key roles for the team included a daily scan of the external environment, identifying changes that would impact on regulatory, and then communicating those changes to the wider regulatory department. This encouraged me to develop a broad awareness of the regulatory environment and, in order to place the regulatory issues in context, a high-level view of the issues facing the pharmaceutical industry.

In addition, regulatory strategists would often ask our team to find information that could help address a specific issue that their product was facing. This provided insights into the work of regulatory strategy and the input that regulatory provides to a product team. A further role was to coordinate the company's response to draft guidance issued by regulatory authorities. This included guidelines for quality, safety, efficacy and the broader regulatory environment, requiring me to work with, and understand the work of, colleagues outside the regulatory department.

After four years in SB's regulatory information team and having taken roles as an Information Manager at *Scrip World Pharmaceutical News* and at a biotech company, I joined Pfizer to be part of its embryonic regulatory information team.

Initially, the role at Pfizer was to develop the RI function. I used my experience from SB to create a valued regulatory intelligence function. The role within Pfizer quickly grew to require more than just gathering and distributing information; the requirements of the regulatory group meant the RI team had to provide additional analyses of the changes and to outline the impact that the changes would have on Pfizer's regulatory strategies and business. Further expansion of the remit added a policy element. This meant that when an external change caused a significant impact, the team has to develop a position on how we would like the environment to be, and identify a series of strategies and tactics that Pfizer could follow to advocate our position externally.

Regulatory policy and intelligence is a niche area for RA. It needs people with an understanding of the contribution from regulatory and the wider environment in which it operates. It also provides opportunities to work across disciplines within your company in addition to external networks with regulators and colleagues working in regulatory across the industry. The external environment is constantly changing, requiring the role of RI to change while providing opportunities to continue learning.

From big pharma to start-up

Alan Newlands, *Vice President Regulatory Affairs, Clovis Oncology, shares some of his career highlights with Angela Miller from Eisai*

Alan Newlands has worked in Regulatory Affairs for over 20 years. He began his career in RA in a very fortunate manner as following his BSc in Genetics, he was sponsored by Pfizer to do a PhD in drug metabolism, and so was exposed to most of the functions within the pharmaceutical industry early on.

Alan comments: 'My first flavour of the industry was working in the drug metabolism labs at Pfizer while I was studying for my PhD. I was aware that there were opportunities outside of the laboratory and after I finished my research, I joined Bayer in their UK RA group. This gave me an excellent grounding in all aspects of pharmaceutical research and development.'

Following his employment at Bayer, Alan then established the European RA function for a Canadian company before joining a pharmaceutical start-up company, Pharmion, where he set up and assumed responsibility not only for all regulatory activities in Europe and all other markets outside of North America but also had responsibility for risk management. 'The role was very rewarding and challenging, particularly as we had thalidomide in our portfolio. I left Pharmion for a well-earned break following an acquisition.'

In this role, Alan considers he was fortunate to have a fantastic team and had the opportunity to interact with many regulators on a global basis. He then worked at Gilead briefly, before taking up his current position in a new start-up company Clovis Oncology as Vice President of Regulatory Affairs.

So what does Alan particularly enjoy about his current position? Well, he says that being in a start-up company means that every day is different and there is a real drive to succeed, a factor that he considers is sometimes lost in big pharmaceutical companies. Consequently, it is a 'great environment to work in as RA is highly regarded and a key element for the successful development of a product'.

But what does he enjoy most about RA? Alan's philosophical about this: 'I enjoy the fact that we interact with all functions and very much see the role as that of a conductor in an orchestra, the legislation and guidelines are the music and we rely on all the functions to perform to bring it all together.'

And are there any negative points? 'It's extremely hard work and can be exhausting, but overall the positives outweigh the negatives. There can be an expectation, particularly in small organisations, to have an immediate answer to every question. The majority of times, we can find out and get it right!'

So would Alan encourage people to consider a regulatory career? 'Absolutely, my view is give it a go, it opens so many doors either within RA or within the industry as a whole. To succeed a science degree is essential; otherwise it can be very challenging understanding the basics. Personality wise, you need a rechargeable battery and the ability to get on well with others.'

Getting on – how professional organisations can help

Participating in the regulatory community

Lynda Wight, *Executive Director, TOPRA*

Scary beginnings

I recall very clearly the instruction I received from my first boss in my first regulatory job in my first week of work at a major pharmaceutical company: 'Fill in this form and join the professional association now, and make sure you take an active part in it.' Admittedly, she had trained under the person that had started the professional body only a few years previously, so perhaps was quite unusual in the level of the support she was showing. But for all that it was possibly the best advice I could have been given. She had taken me on straight from university and I knew next to nothing about regulation of medicines, but she had been so delighted when I had talked about the CSM and yellow card reporting of adverse drug reactions (the sum total of my knowledge) at my interview that she had offered me the job!

I joined the professional body, and immediately went to an event where I met other fresh-faced young graduates starting out on their regulatory careers. I recall the 'disco' at the end of one of the busy days of presentations, sitting shyly with my two new friends and watching the 'great and good' of the regulatory world disport themselves on the dance floor. 'Would we ever know as much as them?' we wondered; admiring them for their regulatory knowledge and confidence, if not their dance moves! Many of these had been the pioneers of the regulatory profession, feeling their way in roles that had only recently been created in response to new legislation, but using that unique position to help shape and influence guidelines and processes that still underpin the modern regulatory system. Some of them are still active as consultants and others became pioneers of regulatory consultancy or education. I was privileged to have been able to learn from them, and they were generous in sharing what they knew with new kids on the block like me: and the same situation pertains today. Those who have learned much in their careers, whether they have worked in companies or government agencies, are willing to share it in the neutral environment of the professional association.

I enrolled on an introductory course, at which I met a host of other new entrants and was relieved to find that I was not the only one struggling to find my way around the legislation or remember how much toxicity testing, and in what species, would be needed to support a clinical trial of 7 days' duration. It made me feel less nervous about the career I had chosen, and more confident that when I had a regulatory problem or an embarrassing gap in my knowledge, there would be other people around whom I could talk to about it. I need no longer fear my Medical Director going on the rampage, needing a water-tight answer to some arcane regulatory point of law IMMEDIATELY – I had a support group who could help. Some of my fellow course attendees are now Vice Presidents of regulatory in major CROs, others work for biotech companies in New Jersey and yet others are running their own businesses in the south of France. And after all these years, I am still in regular contact with them, still gaining support and encouragement and not a little regulatory 'gossip'.

Gaining confidence

Gradually I built up my knowledge and gained more skills that would help me progress in my career. With knowledge gained 'on the job' came confidence and the ability to take greater responsibility in my company. However, ours was a small department, ridiculously so for the size of company. The upside of this was the potential to be involved in a whole range of activities: not just core 'registration' tasks but the wider remit of RA, including adverse event reporting, and literature approval eg. The downside was that the two of us could not know everything and we relied on our external networks to help us when faced with a new problem. Professional training courses gave us not just the technical knowledge, but the practical expertise of the presenters who were willing to share this within their professional 'community'.

As I began to get more experience I was asked to help in the organisation of training meetings and conferences. I started off very much as the new girl on a working party and, as befitted my station, was given the job of 'paraphernalia' which meant that I was responsible for pads and pens and badges. But it did mean I was sitting around a table with people from all walks of regulatory life, who talked about their recent successes (and failures), widened my network and gave me insight on how it might be to work in a different environment when the time came to move on. I must have been really good at pads and pens because I eventually became a Chairman of a working party.

As well as forcing me to look at current technical issues and reach out to those who were the experts in that area to speak and compile the programme, this experience taught me valuable skills that perhaps my job could not: building a team, managing a project to a drop-dead deadline, problem-solving, controlling a budget and encouraging others to deliver their bit. My company work took priority of course, but my employers recognised that I could balance my work for them and my commitments to the profession and could also see the benefits my involvement brought to them. The other side of that coin was that I felt trusted and valued by my employer: they supported my involvement because they recognised me and my role as truly 'professional'.

Flushed with my successes in the training sector I got involved with running a module for the MSc and with editing the journal (a whole new set of skills are needed there)! Each and every one of these projects increased my personal knowledge, introduced me to new people and raised the profile of the company I worked for and of me as a regulatory professional. This latter was to prove particularly useful as my career took a new turn.

Moving on and giving back

The time came for me to try something different in my career and I decided to take a risk and help set up one of the first consultancy companies, with a colleague of mine. It was then that I appreciated the value of the contacts I had made. Those who had met me through my work at the professional association knew that I was active and thus in touch with the latest developments; they had seen evidence of my hard work and commitment and felt that they could trust me as clients. As the company grew, some of them joined me as colleagues; my involvement had reaped benefits for my career in terms of the opportunities and work I was offered.

I maintained my active involvement in the professional association and decided to stand as a Board member, taking on the responsibilities as a company Director at my own company and in the association. By this time I recognised the value of what my years of 'belonging' had given me and wanted to make sure that this possibility existed and indeed was extended for the growing number of regulatory professionals. I had reaped the benefits of having the support of my professional association at a time of great change when the regulatory system moved from a national to a European-based procedure.

Today, those who face changes in advanced therapies, paediatric legislation, scientific advice, pharmacovigilance, HTA and other developments, need that support much more. In the competitive employment environment of today, everyone needs to be the best they can be and belonging to and being involved with TOPRA can help do that. Now TOPRA has a Student member category, those toying with a career in RA can come to it with some knowledge and understanding, perform better at interview and be really ready to impress from day one!

Working in TOPRA today

The profession of RA has developed enormously from those early days and the skills needed by practitioners are more diverse than ever. But the need to be technically up to date, to know how to find out about new developments, to build a network of contacts for support and information-sharing (and new job opportunities) remains. TOPRA now offers a structured 'cradle to grave' training programme, a lifelong learning plan, formal postgraduate qualifications, a peer-reviewed and highly-regarded journal, e-learning opportunities and career coaching – all the resources the RA professional might need to build the technical skills to do well. But it is the friends, colleagues, contacts, networks – call them what you will – that can make the difference between being adequate or being good – and enjoying it too!

Continuing professional development – and LifeLong Learning

Tony Cartwright, *Pharmaceutical Regulatory Consultant, Global Regulatory Solutions and* Craig McCarthy, *Managing Director, CAMPHARM*

What is lifelong learning?

All the major professions ask their members to undertake continuing professional development (CPD). TOPRA calls this LifeLong Learning (LLL). The world of Regulatory Affairs is ever-changing, with new legal requirements, scientific guidelines, procedures and changing formats for regulatory submissions. All of us need to continuously strive to keep up to date, and this is done in a variety of ways.

TOPRA LLL Scheme

TOPRA introduced the LLL Scheme in 2008. All details can be found on the TOPRA website on www.topra.org/lifelong-learning. The TOPRA LLL Scheme is a free toolkit for you to help plan your personal and professional development. It gives you a means of assessing what skills and experience you need to carry out different roles in RA. It also gives managers and senior RA staff a more systematic way to analyse and review the development needs of staff. A record of LLL is far more than just a training record (see below) and it will form an invaluable complement to your CV. If you work in a CRO or a consulting company, clients of the company will particularly value you if you can show them that you are a Registered TOPRA member with a carefully documented record of LLL. When you want to change jobs your LLL record will be invaluable to your new employer.

LLL is much more than just 'training'. It includes any formal training you undertake with TOPRA (such as the Introductory Course and CRED courses) and also any other internal and external courses. But it is much broader and includes:

- Being mentored by a more senior colleague on some aspect of regulatory work
- Consulting the internet for new or existing information and guidelines from the regulatory agencies on procedures, technical requirements for filings, etc
- Consulting the internet for regulatory intelligence (eg, precedents from other companies' submissions)

- Reading technical and professional publications (eg, *Regulatory Rapporteur*)
- Reading books and articles, or undertaking e-courses, about 'soft skills' (eg, influencing, negotiating, decision making) and management
- Preparation of presentations to your work colleagues or for an external conference or training course
- Preparation of an article for publication
- e-Learning from the TOPRA or other websites
- Work-based projects and short-term roles in other departments to gain wider experience
- Voluntary work such as coaching a team which improves interpersonal or leadership skills
- Attending TOPRA Working Party or Committee meetings to discuss policy, plan training courses or conferences
- Attending an industry or regulatory agency working party meeting
- Being coached.

LLL is a tool for you as an RA professional at all stages of your career, from new entrant to the profession to Vice President of Regulatory Affairs in a major company.

How much time should you expect to spend on LLL per year?

When you are at the beginning of your career you need to spend more time on training to get up to speed in your job. You may also need more training if you move into another job or a more specialist area. If you undertake the modular TOPRA MSc course you will probably find you need to spend over 150 hours a year on LLL. TOPRA recommends that overall a reasonable target is 50 to 100 hours a year.

Regulatory 'competences' – what are they

TOPRA has defined a list of competences for RA professionals and you can find these on the LLL section of the TOPRA website. A competence is the knowledge, skills and behaviour which enable effective performance in a specific role or function. You can use this list of competences to ensure that you develop an appropriate range of skills for your job.

For example if you start work in RA doing CTAs or human medicines you will need to develop the competences 'knowledge and application of current procedures for obtaining approval to carry out clinical trials in the European Union' and also 'knowledge and application of current procedures for obtaining approval in other countries as appropriate to carry out clinical trials'. You will also need to have the competence 'knowledge about the discovery and development of pharmaceutical products'.

As you move towards gaining more responsibility in a team responsible for marketing authorisation applications, you will need additional competences such as 'knowledge and application of registration procedures in Europe for MA approvals, variations, extensions and renewals'. And then 'knowledge and application of the technical, chemical, pharmaceutical and biological requirements for registration of chemical entities'. Since the file will need to include the texts for the promotion of the product, you will need to have competence in 'knowledge and application of requirements for information for promotion, labelling', and so on.

By the time you reach the elevated position of Vice President Global Regulatory Affairs you will probably have all of the competences in the TOPRA list!

All of the TOPRA courses/conferences include a mention in the advertising of both the specific competences being covered and the hours of LLL involved.

Soft skills

An important part of any job are the soft skills. Skills such as influencing, communication, team management, delegating, appraising, presenting and motivating are now recognised as key to making businesses more profitable and better places to work. In RA, skills such as those involved in the management and supervision of staff, project management, negotiating skills (both with internal colleagues and with staff from contractors and the regulatory agencies) are needed. In modern pharmaceutical companies much of the work is done in project teams with staff at different levels and from different technical areas. Thus development of soft skills competences is also a vital part of your development.

There are a number of TOPRA e-learning courses available to you covering the broad areas of managing people; HR and compliance; personal effectiveness; professional skills; and sales and marketing. The courses include:

- Negotiation Skills
- Principles of Consultative Selling
- Project Management
- Conducting Performance Appraisals
- Leadership Skills
- Managing High Performing Teams

Identifying your training needs

The TOPRA competences can help you when negotiating with your manager to get the training and development you need. When it comes time for your annual appraisal with your manager, one of the aspects which will be considered is how you will extend your role in the company. You should ask yourself the question 'where do I want to be in one or two years' time?' You should be prepared for the meeting by looking at the TOPRA list of competences, deciding which need covering, and probably how the gaps in your competences can be addressed by means of courses, e-learning, working with other teams, etc. The TOPRA website includes a Personal Learning Plan for you to write down how you want to address your development needs. You may find it useful to do a regular SWOT Analysis (your strengths, weaknesses, opportunities and threats).

Should I keep a record of my LLL?

Remember that no one has a job for life any more, and if there are mergers and acquisitions involving your company, or a lack of opportunity, you need to be fully prepared to move elsewhere with a well-documented portable skill set of relevant competences.

Your company may well keep its own record of any training you and your colleagues undertake. However as we mentioned earlier a training record is not the same as an LLL record, as there are many more areas covered in LLL. A full record of your own LLL will be invaluable to you personally and you could keep it on your own PC at work or at home if the company record is just a training record. If you keep your own LLL record it is much easier to use it to update your CV when you are applying for a new job at the next level.

TOPRA has a suggested format for your LLL record – the LifeLong Learning Log, and there is also an example of a Lifelong Learning Log in the LLL section of its website. However you can keep your record in any way that suits you.

Craig McCarthy, a past President of TOPRA, reflects on the value that LLL has to him as an RA professional with 25-plus years of experience

If I had recorded my LLL at an early stage of my career I would today have a complete record of my career, which would be very valuable. It would cover my regulatory career as a fresh pharmacy graduate starting in the profession to today as a seasoned RA professional who made it to the 'top of TOPRA'. I could have used this LLL record throughout my 25-plus year career, in conjunction with my CV, in a variety of ways, including:

- To gain Registered membership of TOPRA
- To provide a record of training for audits
- In job interviews as a record of my competence
- In annual appraisals to identify professional development needs going forward and to show how my professional development had advanced
- In planning for my own professional development
- To obtain a Fellowship of TOPRA.

However, as my imagination ran away with me on what I could have used the LLL Log for in planning my career in RA in the past, I thought, but what use is it now? The next day I had my answer. I was asked by an auditor of a client to supply them with my training record and CV. Immediately I sent them a reply with my LLL record by e-mail as a PDF. They were astounded and complimented me on my professional approach and were very impressed with the extent of my training and records.

So I am now committed to filling in my LLL regularly and I would encourage every RA professional to go onto the website and make a start at the LLL scheme. Plan your training to match the key competences you require to move to the next stage of your professional career. It may be formal training you need, perhaps the 'gold standard' introductory courses, a practical training course such as CRED, a hot topic meeting on new developments, or the annual symposium for a 'bird's eye view'. It may be a qualification such as the ultimate MSc in RA. But also don't forget to enter all of the 'on the job' training, reading and skills development that you embark on to meet your aims. These can all help you to meet your career aspirations and by starting an LLL habit now you are building up a record for a successful future.

Coaching and mentoring

Susan Botfield, *Certified NLP Trainer and Business Coach, Four Pillars Coaching**

The world of Regulatory Affairs has changed dramatically in the past 10 years and continues to do so. We are faced with balancing increased and ever-changing legislation, increased commercial pressures and unprecedented merger and acquisitions activity, all meaning that RA departments are stretched to capacity. What does this mean for individuals and teams in RA? The 'right first time' philosophy does not just apply to dossier submission. This pressured environment means that we need to apply this philosophy to all our interactions both internal and external.

As Daniel Goleman, the author of *Working with Emotional Intelligence*, says: 'The rules for work are changing. We are judged by a new yardstick: not by how smart we are, or by our training and expertise, but also by how well we handle ourselves and each other. This yardstick is increasingly applied in choosing who will be hired and who will not, who will be let go and who retained, who passed over and who promoted.'

Take a critical view of the job descriptions in your organisation or even your own job description. The first third generally describes the academic or business skills required and the other two-thirds will generally describe the interpersonal and intrapersonal skills expected. It is suggested that one-third of your day is employing your technical or business skills and the rest is spent persuading and influencing people to get the job done.

A coaching and/or mentoring relationship can identify and support your acquisition of advanced listening and oral communication, group and interpersonal effectiveness, active team participation, the motivation to make a difference or contribution and of course increased leadership potential. If leadership is defined as 'the process of social influence in which one person can enlist and support the aid of others in the accomplishment of a common task' then we are all leaders.

Coach or mentor?

An external coach is entirely objective and focused on the goals and development needs of the team or individual being coached. An external coach will be well-qualified in several coaching methods and have knowledge of leadership theory and practice. An external coach will challenge a client's assumptions and ask powerful, relevant questions to support the individual in identifying and implementing a working solution. An external coach will hold the client accountable.

A mentor is generally a business colleague who has the experience you want to gain in both technical and intrapersonal spheres. Sharing technical experience works well but unless the mentor is also a qualified coach they can only offer their own intrapersonal experience and you have one model to follow. Using an external coach to train internal coaches is a successful method of creating a coaching culture.

Skills that we can acquire through a coaching relationship include how to build an effective team especially if transitioning into management for the first time; how to set powerful and achievable goals for yourself and/or others; techniques and strategies for understanding and influencing others; how to give feedback and to create a genuine feedback culture; how to identify and increase self-belief which aids reaching for stretch goals; how to create and manage your career and above all how to communicate all these skills in order to retain and work with the best. Coaching can aid swift refocus and support in leading an individual or a team towards project success. It can consist of a couple of sessions or a development plan for leadership.

Coaching for success

Graduation to RA officer role When coaching an ambitious science graduate keen to get his first break into RA we took a critical review of his CV. He had underplayed the work experience gained throughout his studies. He had various part-time jobs including data entry (accuracy); waiting tables in a 200-seat restaurant (teamwork) and events management experience (projects and people skills). After interview practice he was advised to research RA by looking at the TOPRA website, taking out Student membership, exploring the MHRA website for how drugs are licensed and to learn keywords and terms. He was offered a RA Officer role at a competitive salary with a Fortune 500 company 8 weeks post-graduation. One session of 1.5 hours.

Non-performing colleague I worked with a newly promoted manager with a team of four of which one RA officer was not performing to potential. We discussed whether the problem was at the level of the team/job environment, behavioural, capabilities or confidence/belief issues. Once realising the issue was seated at the confidence level we discussed using the Hersey Blanchard situational leadership model to first guide (show and tell), then coach, support and finally let the RA officer fly solo on a piece of work with great results for the whole team. One session of 1.5 hours.

Dealing with a personality clash Working with a Senior RA officer we discussed how to get some forward movement in a work relationship that she described as toxic. We worked together using a technique to give three different perspectives on the same situation during which she gained a deeper understanding of the intentions of both herself and the other party. This reflective exercise gave her the motivation to discuss the matter openly with her colleague and they achieved a more congenial working atmosphere. One session of 1 hour.

Building a team Working with a manager after an internal restructure and a new team of five was a challenge for four meetings. We discussed two models of team development, and how the manager would behave to help the team work through the development stages to really working together. We worked on preparing and managing meetings, also ensuring that all team members had the chance to contribute. Much discussion centred on encouraging but containing healthy conflict and arriving at solutions that motivated the whole team. The result gave the manager an effective team in a pressured environment more quickly than expected. Four meetings of 1.5 hours.

In conclusion

Whether you are aiming to get your first regulatory role or want to discuss building your career plans it is worthwhile considering whether to seek help from a coach or a mentor. At company interviews your ability to convey in one hour, that you have the basic technical and interpersonal skills to deal with the complexities of this profession will be paramount. It often helps to practise and gain some external support whether from tutors, colleagues or experts in this field.

*Four Pillars coaching offers TOPRA members a complimentary 30 minute telephone coaching session or a free review of your CV in addition to an objective appraisal of your current situation.

Glossary of terms used in this booklet

AFSSAPS	Agence Francaise de Securite Sanitaire des Produits de Sante
BPD	Biocidal Products Directive
BPR	Biocidal Products Regulations
CMC	Chemistry, Manufacturing and Controls
CPD	Continuing Professional Development
CRO	Contract Research Organisation
CSM	Committee for the Safety of Medicines
CTA	Clinical Trial Application
CVMP	Committee for Veterinary Medicinal Products
eCTD	electronic Common Technical Document
EDQM	European Directorate for the Quality of Medicines
EMA	European Medicines Agency
FDA	Food and Drug Administration
HA	Health Authority
HSE	Health and Safety Executive
HTA	Health Technology Assessment
IND	Investigational New Drug
LLL	LifeLong Learning
MA	Marketing Authorisation
MDD	Medical Devices Directive
MHRA	Medicines and Healthcare Regulatory Authority
NCE	New Chemical Entity
RA	Regulatory Affairs
R&D	Research and Development
RI	Regulatory Intelligence
SOP	Standard Operating Procedure

TOPRA as a career resource

TOPRA is the global organisation for Regulatory Affairs professionals and for those who have an interest in Regulatory Affairs in the healthcare sector. Our members are based in over 40 countries and they are drawn from industry, the regulatory agencies and the consultancy community, working in all sectors including medical technologies, biotech, borderline products and pharmaceuticals.

Training and development

TOPRA is a non-profit, non-political organisation which seeks to advance the status of the regulatory profession through education, and provision of information to its members. Members have the advantage of a structured training programme available to them at preferential rates. This programme ranges from intensive Introductory Courses for new entrants to the profession, through detailed practical courses on topics of interest to those with a few years' experience, to an MSc qualification. There are also management courses designed specifically to meet the challenges of the regulatory professional as his or her career develops. The training programmes are highly regarded and internationally recognised in the RA profession.

Information resources

Members have access to *Regulatory Rapporteur*, an international journal covering regulatory developments and www.topra.org which offers a full range of regulatory news, industry links and career opportunities to list but a few.

Useful reading on careers

Alternative Careers in Science: Leaving the Ivory Tower (Scientific Survival Skills) (2nd edition) edited by Cynthia Robbins-Roth, Elsevier Academic Press, 2006.

Careers with the Pharmaceutical Industry (2nd edition) edited by Peter D Stonier, published by John Wiley & Sons, 2003.

Career Opportunities in Biotechnology and Drug Development by Toby Fredman, Cold Spring Harbor Laboratory Press, 2008.

Other useful books

For a general introduction to EU RA try *Evaluating Medicines – Perspectives from a European Regulatory Authority* edited by DS Slijkerman *et al*, TOPRA Publishing, 2010.

For an in-depth industry review, borrow *International Pharmaceutical Product Registration* (2nd edition) edited by Anthony C Cartwright and Brian R Matthews, Informa Healthcare, 2009, which should be available via your university library.